T0149750

TEN GREAT CHRISTIAN SERMONS

Volume I

DR. JOHN THOMAS WYLIE

authorHOUSE®

AuthorHouse™
1663 Liberty Drive
Bloomington, IN 47403
www.authorhouse.com
Phone: 1 (800) 839-8640

King James Version (KJV)
Public Domain

New International Version (NIV)
Holy Bible, New International Version˚, NIV˚ Copyright ©1973, 1978, 1984, 2011 by Biblica, Inc.˚ Used by permission. All rights reserved worldwide.

Revised Standard Version (RSV)
Revised Standard Version of the Bible, copyright © 1946, 1952, and 1971 the Division of Christian Education of the National Council of the Churches of Christ in the United States of America. Used by permission. All rights reserved.

New American Standard Bible (NASB)
Copyright © 1960, 1962, 1963, 1968, 1971, 1972, 1973, 1975, 1977, 1995 by The Lockman Foundation

Published by AuthorHouse 06/08/2018

ISBN: 978-1-5462-4636-7 (sc)
ISBN: 978-1-5462-4635-0 (e)

Print information available on the last page.

CONTENTS

PREFACE

Preaching is the announcement of the message of God. It generally has been the God designated method for engendering the good news of Jesus Christ. The messenger Paul expressed: "It pleased God by the foolishness of preaching to save them that believe" (I Cor. 1:21). I reason that "It's Preaching Or Nothing." Soon after I was called to the Gospel Ministry in June 1979, I started perusing a few sermons of numerous extraordinary evangelists while likewise matriculating at the American Baptist Theological Seminary of the American Baptist College. I understood that a sermon is preferred being heard over being read. I perceived that perusing a large group of sermons won't change your life. One must react to what is perused with a faithful heart to the standards of God's assertion and permit the Holy Spirit to apply reality to your life.

I have a conviction that in nowadays and times, profoundly, we should preach more sermons on the considerable truths of the Christian Faith.

In the meantime, we should preach sermons in the easiest terms conceivable so that lay person in the pew can get it. I have attempted to achieve this perfect in this book.

I trust these "Ten Great Christian Sermons" might be utilized by my kindred brethren to favor numerous hearts.

All Scriptures are taken from the Authorized King James Version of the Bible and are the author's own sermons. No other references are made in the bibliography save God's inspired Word.

Reverend Dr. John Thomas Wylie

SERMON

ONE

The Lord's Last Invitation
(Revelation 22:17)

"And The Spirit and the bride say, come. And let Him that heareth say, come. And let him that is athrist come. And whosoever will, let him take the water of life freely."

Numerous years back, when I was younger, I had passed old summary houses which were censured properties. A colossal sign was posted on the front passageway which said: "Keep Out."

I have seen signs on office doors which said: "Private, No Admission..."

I have seen other signs which warned: "Restricted Area, Keep Out."

In this world, there are signs that say all kinds of things but that is man's way; while God's way is quite different.

The Lord's way opens every door and says to the sinner: "Come in and be saved." "Come in and enjoy all I have for you."

God's great purpose in redemption is clear unto all humanity.

Human kind is lost in transgression. God gave his lone Son to recover them, and now He welcomes everybody to come to Him through Jesus Christ and be spared (saved).

This point keeps running all through the Bible like a running stream through a valley. In Isaiah 55:1 we read:

"Ho, every one that thirsteth, come ye to the waters, and he that hath no money; come ye, buy, and eat; yea, come, buy wine and milk without money and without price."

In Isaiah 1:18 we Read: "Come now, and let us reason together, saith the Lord: Though your sins be as scarlet, They shall be white as snow; Though they be red like crimson, they shall be as wool."

In Matthew 11:28, Jesus said: "Come unto me, all ye that labour and are heavy laden, and I will give you rest." In John 6:37 Jesus said: "Him that cometh to me I will in no wise cast out."

In our text, John, The Beloved Apostle was in exile on the Isle Of Patmos; and God uses John to write The Book Of Revelation. Just as John is about to close the book out: "wait a minute, don't close yet. Don't put down your pen 'til I give one more urgent invitation to sinners.

John! Try not to finish off the book; til again I can welcome heathens to desire salvation. God might welcome you today. Maybe, God is giving you one more chance to come to Christ.

The Holy Spirit welcomes the heathen to come. The primary work of the Holy Spirit in the human heart is to convict men of wrongdoing and point them to the Lamb of God who is Jesus Christ. It is He who achieves apology and confidence in our salvation. The individuals who are spared can recollect how the Holy Spirit made them see their wrongdoing and swing to Jesus Christ.

At the point when Jesus met Paul on the Damascus Road: He said to Paul - "It is hard for thee to kick against the pricks." What were these pricks? Like a sharp stick pricking the tissue the Holy Spirit was pricking Paul. Regularly, The Holy Spirit kept in Paul's psyche the substance of Stephen, passing on for Christ, and his face sparkling with radiant light. He couldn't make tracks in an opposite direction from these pricks.

The individuals who have not given their lives to Christ: You have encountered sharp blows on your inner voice. You recollect your dad's or mom's confidence and when they kicked the bucket, how you guaranteed to change your life. At the point when another adored one kicked the bucket; you guaranteed to change your life and live for Him, yet you are yet to keep that promise.

You recall how God has blessed you abundantly over the years and how you said: "I ought to stay in the church." "I ought to be a different person."

Yes! The Holy Spirit touches us in various ways. Be that as it may, Remember: He said my Spirit might not generally endeavor with man. The threat in promising God you will change and never give your life to Jesus Christ is that He may lift His hand from your inner voice and let you go on your approach to hellfire. Things being what they are, at this moment: Why not hear Him while He is calling and acknowledge Christ as Your Lord and Savior?

The Church of the Lord welcomes you to come. The Bible says in Revelation 22:17, "The lady of the hour welcomes you." The Bride is the congregation and each genuine church is calling delinquents to contrition and salvation. The essential mission of the congregation is to get out delinquents. Welcome them to come to Jesus Christ and to live for Christ. The principle errand of the congregation is to win souls. Every one of us can't lecture, sing or educate, yet every christian ought to welcome a lost soul to Christ. The Church, (Christ's Bride) Invites you to come.

The Heavenly City welcomes you to come.

In Revelation, that sublime city or blessed city is portrayed as descending out of paradise. That grand city calls for us to get through it's doors. You know church, in each man and in each lady there is a hunger (a yearning). A hunger or a yearning for rest, peace, and delights of satisfaction that can be discovered just in that magnificent city.

We sing: swing low, sweet chariot, seeking to convey me home. Individuals need to go where there is no neediness, no affliction, no passing, no distress, no tears, no broken hearts or broken homes. Paradise is that spot which calls us to come to Jesus: so that some time or another we may live there in that magnificent home.

The Outcast can come through Christ and get to be Christlike.

The heathen can turn into a holy person, The

Drunkard can get to be calm, the medication someone who is addicted can turn out to be perfect, the poor can get to be prosperous, and the terrible can get to be unadulterated.

Yes, Heaven calls you to come to Jesus Christ.

Everybody who hears God's Word is to welcome others to come.

Let him that heareth say, come. The Holy Spirit calls, The Church calls, The Heavenly Home calls.

Furthermore, The Lord God says to everybody who hears - take the message and tell another person.

The Lord has said: "Let him that is athirst come." What God is stating to us is:

'That everybody who is worn out on a wicked life and is disappointed with life and its delights; and needs peace in their heart; to come!

Zacchaeus, who climbed a sycamore tree to see Jesus was parched. The publican who shouted out: "God be benevolent to me a miscreant, was parched. The wicked lady who came to Jesus at the well was parched. The World is brimming with parched individuals.

The issue is they're attempting to extinguish their thirst at the wells of the world.

Give us a chance to envision for a minute that a gathering of men are lost in the desert. They stagger and fall, looking for water. Their tongues are hanging out as their quality debilitates under the rankling sun. Some can scarcely pause and fall by the wayside. At that point, one of the men see a pool of water. They all hurry to the pool of water and toss themselves down and drink until they are fulfilled. In the desert it is valuable to at last discover a beverage of water, when one is verging on kicking the bucket of thirst. Physical thirst is awful profound thirst is far more awful.

You might be profoundly parched yet you don't need to lurch or tumble down to look for a wellspring off water. That wellspring is adjacent. Jesus is the water of life you look for. Come and drink of Him. Jesus satisfies each thirst of the human soul.

John 3:16 peruses: "For God so cherished the world, that He gave His lone sired Son, that whosoever believeth in Him ought not die, but rather have endless life." In John 3:16, The Whosoever is welcome to come. The Whosoever will is a welcome stretched out and salvation offered to anybody, everybody and anyone.

Jesus said, "In my father's home are numerous mansions." as it were, there is bounty great room in my father's kingdom for you! For whosoever will come to Christ. The Whosoever incorporates everybody. It makes the same to God you ethnic foundation, race, for God acknowledges you whether you are dark or white, yellow or chestnut or red, Rich or Poor, High or low; God cherishes all individuals. He welcomes all to come yet few have searched for Him. God cherishes all humankind and holds his arms completely open in adoring welcome for you to come to Him through his Beloved Son, Jesus Christ. Who so ever leaves the old life and takes after Jesus can be spared unto salvation.

What is the invitation? It is to take of the water of Life.

Jesus gives the water to you; however it is dependent upon you to take the water He gives you.

When you are to a great degree wiped out, the specialist offers you solution. You take prescription for pressing sicknesses on the grounds that on the off chance that you don't take your pharmaceutical, your disease could deteriorate and cause you your life.

When you are profoundly wiped out we call it being sin wiped out. When you are sin debilitated Jesus, the considerable doctor offers you the main solution for transgression disorder of a lost soul. You take what the Lord brings to the table or you may kick the bucket in trespasses and sin. You don't need to pass on in an unsaved condition on the off chance that you take of this water which Jesus offers; for you sins will be totally pardoned.

Your heart will be changed. Your spirit will be spared, and your brain will be a made up psyche to serve the Lord. You will pick up a companion who sticks nearer than a sibling! You'll be en route to paradise rather than hellfire.

In life - If you need to have anything worth anything, we need to work at it. Be that as it may, I am happy today that salvation is free. You don't work for salvation. Paradise is free and salvation is free. Jesus Christ is allowed to all who will come to Him.

On Calvary's Cross He paid the cost for our salvation. He paid it with His life and the shedding of His Blood more than 2,000 years prior. God came in the individual of Jesus Christ to bite the dust for our wrongdoings, to kick the bucket in our place. Jesus came to look for, to discover, to spare what is lost.

This welcome the Lord amplifies is salvation for the individuals who acknowledge it. On the off chance that you don't have any acquaintance with him today you would be advised to discover who he is! He is Jesus Christ who's ready to spare you. Have you attempted him? He can spare the most astounding, He can spare the least. I am happy I can tell the world He's trust in a sad world.

This is the Lord's last welcome and it could be somebody's last chance to acknowledge Christ. In the event that I were lost, I get in a rush. No big surprise the hymn writer thought of this might be the last time. This might be the last chance to get right with the Lord. I don't think about you however I need to be in the place my Jesus is. I need to go to that residence of the Lord, from whence came Christ, and to which place He returned. Don't you need to go to that spot called heaven in the sky? Don't you need to go to the home of the holy people? Don't you need to go to that enveloping sky? I need to go to that spot where there is joy. The spot saved for the equitable. The spot where we'll all be accumulated around God's throne. Where our names will be composed in the Lamb's Book of Life.

SERMON

TWO

There's No Person Like Jesus
(Matthew 1:20-21)

"But while He thought on these things, behold, the angel of the Lord appeared unto Him in a dream; saying, Joseph, Thou Son of David, Fear not to take unto thee Mary thy wife: for that which is conceived in her is of the Holy Ghost (v.20)." "And she shall bring forth a Son, and thou shalt call His name Jesus: for he shall save his people from their sins (v.21)."

We want to focus our attention on the middle half of verse 21. It reads:

"Thou shalt call His name Jesus."

Jesus is one who has a widespread Personality. History makes such a case. Jesus is the one Subject for the evangelist. Jesus is the one noteworthy sympathy toward the congregation. Jesus is the main trust in a transgression wiped out world. The immense predictions of the Bible point to Him; while the eyes of the world are centered around Him. There is no person like Jesus.

Around him the contemplations of the world rotates. In Jesus, the salvation of the world pivots. From Jesus, the light of the world transmits. Through Jesus the severity of life are made sweet. In Jesus all life is based on Him. From Jesus there streams all force. Through Jesus another life is given and the old life kicks the bucket. By Jesus, the delinquent is unshackled from the chains of lostness. There is no individual like Jesus.

"Who is Like unto thee, 'O Lord?" There is nobody like the Lord Jesus! He's God and He's God independent from anyone else!

It is Jesus who lifts us from the weight of wrongdoing. It is Jesus who disperses the shadows of death. No one but Jesus can lift the heap of judgment from our shoulders. It is Jesus who changes our blurring would like to fadeless grandness. Just Jesus opens entryways that no man can close and just Jesus makes an exit from no chance.

It is Jesus who will meet us toward the end of life's Journey. Only he warms the cold waters and holds our hand oblivious hours of death There is no individual like Jesus.

Who is like unto Thee, 'O, Lord? From everlasting to everlasting, Thou Art God! Without him, there is no other. Jesus alone is Holy!

This tells us something about His personal character. It lets us know Jesus is perfect, stainless, He is righteous, without spot or flaw. His life is one perfectly clear; as well as Purer than the purest. Now and again, when His adversaries attempted to trap Him and blame Him for wrongdoing, Jesus said to His foes: "Which of you convinceth Me of transgression?"

There is no character in all the volumes of writing, history, analyzes or plays that may be equivalent to Jesus.

Some society today put Jesus in the rundown of names close by what some should seriously think about goo men: naming great men as His associates. In any case, I come to let you know that Jesus doesn't have any associates. For Jesus alone is the supreme King of rulers and Lord of masters. Jesus alone is the incomparable character all through time, history and time everlasting.

Jesus' character can not be contrasted and anybody. Jesus alone is the Alpha and the Omega, the start of everything and all things. Jesus alone is outright however last. He is the otherworldly Goliath for all time, all others are smaller people. Accordingly, Jesus is conclusion in character.

On one event, when John the Baptist was placed in jail, he sent word to Jesus asking-would you say you are the person who ought to come, Or would it be a good idea for us to search for another? The Christian world since John's opportunity stops to pose that question.

We have had extraordinary men in the different fields of concentrate, yet we search for others. We've had awesome scholars, for example, Plato, Aristotle, Hegel and Kant but still we search for others. We've been enchanted by the considerable writers, for example, Dante, Shakespeare and Giovanni yet despite everything we search for others. We have had our incredible researchers like Galileo and Newton who have made extraordinary commitments yet despite everything we search for others. We have had our incredible statesmen, for example, Lincoln, Washington, Johnson, Kennedy, Clinton and Obama, however despite everything we search for others.

We've had awesome ministers like Franklin, Daniels, Moody, King however we search for others. Our reality has been honored by the lives of good men, for example, Abraham, Issac, Jacob, James, John, and David, however we search for others. Numerous awesome flaring, smoldering prophets visioned the future and sounded their trumpets such men as Isaiah, Jeremiah, Ezekiel and Daniel, yet we search for one who could and revealed God's affection to humankind. We searched for one who could convey us from the jail place of transgression. Jesus is the since quite a while ago searched for one. Presently, since we have Jesus, we don't have to search for any other individual. Why? I am fulfilled by Jesus alone! Just Jesus has a heavenly character. He was sent from God. Jesus bore the picture of God. He is God incarnate (The God man). his character surpasses the nature of character found in all others. There is no individual like Jesus!

He surpassed Abraham in steadfastness. Jesus surpassed Job in tolerance and in devotion. He surpassed Solomon in insight and Elijah in intensity. Jesus surpassed Jeremiah in reason and Melchizedek in enormity. He surpassed Peter in strength and John in dedication. He surpassed James in faithfulness and Paul in preacher enthusiasm; the most conciliatory in penance. There is no individual like Jesus!

There is none similar to Him in force! His energy was showed in creation. The Bible says: "All things were made by Him; and without Him was not anything made that was made." His energy is found in His capacity to spare souls. Wherefore He can spare them to the furthest that come unto God by Him. Jesus is the world's exclusive Savior. There is no individual like Jesus!

Just Jesus has the ability to look for, find and spare that which is lost. John voiced it along these lines: "He said Behold, The Lamb of God; which taketh away the wrongdoing of the world."

Today, we live in a world that is ravenous and sin-wiped out. A world that is destined and sad. A world that is injured and dying, dull and lost. A world that asks an age old inquiry: "In whom should we go?"

As Christians, we should guide them to Jesus Christ. There's no individual like Jesus! Jesus alone is capable for He said, "My beauty is adequate." Jesus alone has the expressions of everlasting life. In his individual, we see the man Jesus, however we likewise see the interminable I Am that I Am. In Jesus we see 100% man and 100% God. As a man Jesus was conceived of a virgin lady, yet as God His soul showed. As a man He ate, drank and dozed, however as God; His Word duplicated 2 fish and 5 pieces sustaining more than 5,000 hungry society. As a man He dozed in Peter's pontoon, yet as God he reprimanded the wind and the waves; quieting the seething tempest; when He said "Peace, Be Still."

As a man He was tempted in all points like us, but as God He ran the devil out of a crazy man. As a man He cried at Lazarus grave, but as God He brought Lazarus back to life again. There is no person like Jesus! As a man he was persecuted but as God He forgives all sin. As a man Jesus was put to death, crucified on the old rugged cross, but as God His agony dying shook the whole earth: opened up graves and dead folk lived again. As a man Jesus was buried in a tomb but as God He did rise again from the dead. He rose up victoriously with power over death, hell and the grave.

As a man He met His disciples in the hills of Galilee but as God He commissioned them to go out win the lost souls in His name. As a man he led them to Bethany but as God He went back to Heaven as Lord of lords and King of kings.

I am glad that His name is the sweetest name that I know. I heard the Bible say: His name shall endure. His name is above every name. His name shall be called Wonderful, Counselor, The mighty God, The

Everlasting Father; The Prince of Peace. His name Alpha and Omega, Beginning and End.

Jesus is my Bright and Morning Star, my Captain of Zion's ship, my Chief Cornerstone. He's a friend to the friendless, and a Father to the fatherless. There's no person like Jesus for He is my Governor, my Good shepherd, and provider.

He is our High Priest of souls and the Great Head of the church.

Somebody said, He's the offspring of David and the Only Begotten Son of God, my redeemer who loves and lives for ever more. He's my way maker, my Great Physician who never lost a patient in Salvation's Hospital. He is my rock in a weary land and water when my soul gets thirsty. Jesus is bread when I get hungry. Jesus is The Way, The Truth and The Light of my life when I need guidance! Do you know Him? There's none other like Him.

Jesus is the Rose of Sharon, my water in dry places, He's my lily of the valley and my wheel in the middle of a wheel. Only Jesus' is the fairest among Ten Thousand. It is Jesus who is Able! He Able!

SERMON

THREE

The Magnetic Drawing Power Of God
(John 12: 30-32)

"Jesus answered and said: This voice came not because of me, But for your sakes (v.30)." "Now is the judgment of this world: Now shall the Prince of this world be cast out (v.31)." "And I, If I be lifted lifted up from the earth, will draw all men unto me (v.32)."

It is said that a magnet is a metal stone fit for drawing in other metal articles. As it were, deductively, a magnet has the ability to attract certain item to itself. We frequently call this attractive force. On the social request of things, it is surely understood that individuals additionally are polarize to each other. That is to say, an individual engaging quality to somebody which appears to attract one near another person, for example, a romance between a man and a lady. Now and again different individuals are polarized by specific gatherings of individuals who share a shared objective, bond or perfect. They are drawn together by the solid individual impact of the gathering also a few teacher and christian church bunches; and additionally a large group of other advantageous associations who are charged or drawn together for the benefit of all of all humankind.

Today, we need to discuss another kind of attraction: The attractive drawing force of God. Here in our content, God attracts our consideration regarding an otherworldly condition or recommendation made by Jesus himself, about Himself, and about Himself. Jesus said, If I be lifted up from the earth, will draw all men unto me. These words talked when Jesus had come to Jerusalem on Monday amid the enthusiasm week. Jesus had about faced to Bethany late Sunday evening; in the wake of having been given an intricate applause from the normal individuals in Jerusalem. He may have stayed at Mary, Martha, and Lazarus home; or in the home of Simon the untouchable.

Early Monday morning Jesus was strolling on His way back to Jerusalem for he had no transportation. He had crashed into Jerusalem that Sunday on another man's donkey. Actually he was sent to another man's cross and covered in another man's grave. He Rose up out the grave for another man's salvation.

On the off chance that you recall, Jesus was strolling that morning since he had halted and reviled a fig tree yet when Jesus had left the fig tree; he then went to the Temple in Jerusalem. While there at the Temple, he set the house all together. He said, He that loveth his life might lose it and he that hateth his life in this world should keep it unto life unceasing.

Presently, in this same message comes our content: "An I, in the event that I be lifted up from the earth, will draw all men unto me." Jesus attracting all men to Him is the attractive drawing force of God. You know church, Power can be negative fascination or a positive fascination.

From a negative perspective force has made some great society turn terrible on the grounds that they couldn't and did not know how to handle a lot of force. Power has transformed honest men into lying men and has brought on some society who held high good norms to stoop lower than the dust. Control now and again causes genuine men to end up hoodlums. Power has made calm men boozers and wine heads. Power has made straight men turn screwy. No individual is sufficiently astute to be trusted with boundless force. Power has been know not homes and plunge families, pulverize countries and gap places of worship. Influence haws turn into the rich man's god and the lawmaker's companion. Power has driven this world to the lost express that it's in. Power has driven this world to the edge of obliteration. These focuses are taking a gander at force from a negative perspective.

In any case, If there is a negative perspective, there must be a positive perspective. At the point when force is looked upon from a positive viewpoint, one can concede that force can be utilized for good and is an extraordinary advantage to all. Mechanical force causes flying machine to rapidly get us from on spot to another.

It is the force of insight that brought about men like Dr. King and other extraordinary pioneers to settle on choices which cleared the street of chance for us. It is the force of information that causes our researchers to perform incredible accomplishment. Political Power has made awesome statesmen and incredible presidents. Athletic power had made awesome athletes in the games field. It is the force of fearlessness that has brought on men and ladies to ascend in America and express their yearning for equivalent rights, human rights, for opportunity and their Constitutional rights. it is the force of affection that has kept homes, church and groups together. No big surprise the author said: "Blest be the tie that ties our hearts in christian love that partnership of related personalities resemble to that.

Presently, Jesus is stating all force has a place with me. What's more, I, on the off chance that I be lifted up from the earth, will draw all men unto me. Jesus was showing an otherworldly truth to an ill-equipped world. The individuals who remained around Him were not readied. His devotees needed to bind this christian religion and energy to Judaism. There were other people who did not oblige Jesus. The Pharisees, did not oblige Jesus. The Sadducees, did not oblige Jesus. Jesus dismissed their unfitness and the ineptness and said: "And I, in the event that I be lifted up from the earth; will draw all men unto me." The demise of Jesus of Jesus removed Him from the dejection of his unapproachable radiance, and associated Him with the entire human race.

The Bible pronounces: "The wages of transgression is demise." Through Jesus passing another life has turned into the gift for some souls. Jesus realized that on the off chance that I be lifted up on a cross, men and ladies, young men and young ladies would get salvation being attracted to Jesus.

Jesus realized that man was lost and at a separation from God; yet Jesus is the Master of separation. It is through Jesus that men will be drawn; that men will be impacted to begin inside and work without. To begin without to work inside is thinking however to begin inside and work without is confidence.

In God's project there must be confidence! For thinking will let us know that 2 fishes and 5 chunks won't bolster 5,000. In any case, confidence lets us know that the eager group moved nearer to Jesus. Jesus take 2 fish and 5 chunks and nourished 5,000 other than ladies and youngsters. Thinking lets us know that a virgin can't conceive an offspring, yet confidence tells approaches us is anything too hard for God. There is nothing unthinkable with Jesus! Jesus said: And I, on the off chance that I be lifted up from the earth, will draw all men unto me. He was lifted up for a lost and fallen mankind. This lifting Him up defended what

Moses had done. God is drawing men unto Himself.

It was God who was attracting Abraham to Himself. Yes! Abraham was drawn by God and did not know where he was going, but rather was in quest for an area who's manufacturer and producer is God. God made Abraham father of the devoted. It was the attractive drawing force of God that drew Jacob as he grapple with the blessed messenger and through Jacob Israel was given her name. I heard it was the drawing force of God that conveyed and drove Moses and Israel out of Pharaoh's hand. Whenever Moses and the offspring of Israel were caught at the Red ocean; Pharaoh's armed force followed them. The general population needed to contend with Moses: Have you driven us around here in the wild amazing there were no graves in Egypt? All things considered, Moses moved nearer to God. God made Moses an incredible deliverer of his kin. Moses said Israel you will see Pharaoh's armed force no more. Simply stop and see the salvation of the Lord. The Lord will do fight for us. Moses extended his bar and oceans isolated and Israel crossed over to the next side while Pharaoh's armed force suffocated in the ocean. God gave Moses the law (Ten Commandments).

Joshua moved nearer to the Lord and the dividers of Jericho came tumbling down. Yes! Extraordinary things can happen when you are gravitated toward to God. There's no force like the Magnetic drawing force of God!

That same force, that same power draws us together in christian unity. That same power draws us closer to Jesus and challenges us to take a closer walk with Him. That Magnetic drawing power of God draws us closer to Him to do the work of the church. The Lord is calling for us not only to be saved but to draw ever closer to him.

It is Jesus' power that will see us through and do what no other power can do.

SERMON

FOUR

Why Jesus Is Not Forgotten
(Matthew 9:4-6)

"And Jesus knowing their thoughts said, wherefore think ye evil in your hearts?" (v.4) "For whether is easier, to say, thy sins be forgiven thee; or to day; arise, and walk?" (v.5) "But that ye may know that The Son of Man hath power on earth to forgive sins, (then saith he to the sick of the palsy,) arise, take up thy bed, and go unto thine house (v.6)."

Today our reality has developed so acclimated to one of its most abnormal occasions as to view it as customary. This occasion is the Remembrance of Jesus. Amid this period ever, Jesus is not generally known. His service finished off in what resembled a miserable annihilation. He Published no original copies or books, he composed no institution of higher learning. He established no administration. Jesus abandoned none of those things by which the popularity is kept from rot. There is not even a genuine picture of Jesus to keep his memory. However, nobody is so well respectfully recognized as Jesus Christ.

Around 1,900 years have passed by; however

Jesus of Nazareth has not been overlooked. Today, millions call him Lord and Savior. Today, His heavenly popularity is more secure than that of any individual who has ever been perceived history. Jesus Christ is our God! Also, on the grounds that this is valid, the heavenly gets to be normal. I see how Jesus did what the sacred writings recorded of him. I am not astounded by what has been going on from that point forward.

We have a clarification of the sublime accomplishments of the early teaches. We ought not be shocked that these supporters of Christ confronted detainment without apprehension; and that the gospel on their lips; frail men they were, yet in Jesus name they flipped around the world.

Salvation has come to us not by some ideology. Jesus did not have faith in a statement of faith. He said: "take up thy cross and take after me..." Anyone may com to Jesus for it is Jesus who offers come to me and tail me.

At to begin with, the supporters of Jesus saw just his human side. At that point, later on as these pupils came to know Jesus better the cover lifted and those same supporters saw God. Give us a chance to get Jesus for all that

He is - for he is God. We should recognize Him in our lives for whatever he can accomplish for us. Jesus alone can do what no other force can do! We can figure out how to know Jesus by living Him. It is Jesus who offers himself to us at the fellowship table; however he offers himself to us in the greater part of life's worries. He comes to us in the time when our needs are closest. Jesus binds himself to our human instinct; that as well as He binds himself to us in otherworldly nature that he may know us and that we may know him.

'As we tail him and render him administration, as we attempt to resemble him, the light of his soul breaks through to us; and on the sacrificial stone of our souls: we declare "that thou workmanship the Christ, the Son of the Living God." Jesus is not overlooked on the grounds that we love him in the grave demonstration of love.

When we watch the Lord's dinner we are doing what Jesus instructed in the times of his service. Jesus said: "This do in remembrance of Me." The memory of Jesus has stayed in the psyches of millions since that forlorn night when he instituted The Lord's Supper. The clock of time has struck at no hour from that point forward that has found the earth unfilled of the considered Jesus.

In each area where Christianity has gone; The Lord's Supper is kept. 'Regardless of what has been the conventions of the general population, regardless of who their saints have been in this world there is a name over each name. It is the name of Jesus - sweetest name we know.

The Rich and the poor have drank from measure of wine which speaks to his shed blood for the abatement of sins. The high and the low have eaten together from the same chunk which speaks to his body which held tight Calvary.

We have bowed at one sacrificial stone in kinship serving Jesus and in this way; make peace. In some cases even with the most exceedingly awful and hardest restriction, we discovered genuine feelings of serenity when we watched the Lord's Supper.

In old times and early phases of Christianity numerous Christians were spooky by mistreatment, driven out of their homes into the night. Despite everything they stayed consistent with Christ. They said: "We will chance all, we will lose all even our lives; yet we will never forget Christ. We will recall that Him as he has told us in the recognition of the Lord's Supper. Why is Jesus not overlooked? Why is he so well and affectionately recalled. It's not on the grounds that he asked us! He asked it, however different pioneers solicited things from their devotees; and they have for quite some time been overlooked!

There were different things which Jesus asked of his devotees and his supporters left them fixed. Jesus is not recollected as a result of his beginning. Jesus birth was superb and phenomenal as we see it today however numerous society amid Jesus life time thought nothing about his introduction to the world. In this way, his introduction to the world does not keep the world entranced for a long time. It is not for the wonders which Jesus played out that he is recalled. The world get energized over supernatural occurrences at first yet overlooks them in a week's chance. It is not a direct result of Jesus teachings that his memory is kept alive! For in the event that we glance surrounding us numerous people do recognize him not to mention take after his teachings. Jesus was the world's most noteworthy educator yet individuals don't venerate instructors. There is something more in Jesus and about him which is more noteworthy than anything he taught. Jesus is not recalled just by his misery. There was his holiest hour when Jesus endured. In the Lord's Supper we see the affliction hireling. However, not even his torment makes him recollected, for there are numerous who remain unaware of Jesus enduring.

Out of all we have expressed to this point about Jesus he is associated with a reason a long ways past all these! Jesus is not overlooked in light of the fact that only he has the force on earth to pardon sin.

Jesus is the special case who can put a crushed down soul spirit on its feet. A hefty portion of us realize this is genuine in light of the fact that he has recuperated our injured broken spirits. Jesus is the special case who brings bliss where there was misery and happiness where there was distress! No one but Jesus can open visually impaired eyes of a man without vision. A significant number of us have been there! Just Jesus can open a hard of hearing ear to hear and get the gospel. No one but Jesus can tear away the cover of uncertainty and skepticism which pieces ones approach to comprehension. No one but Jesus can convey deliverance to an incapacitated will and make his will your will. No one but Jesus can free the chains of insidiousness doing in one's heart and fill it with adoration which streams from heart to heart and bosom to bosom. No one but Jesus can summon from the grave of hopelessness a dead soul in trespasses and in wrongdoing. No one but Jesus can spare one's spirit. This is not on the grounds that he guaranteed it in light of the fact that any religion can make a guarantee of salvation. That is to say, any religion may guarantee salvation after death; yet Jesus has guaranteed to spare us before death, through death, and after death. No one but Jesus can spare you on earth.

This is the place Jesus go to the throne. The world can guess as it will about the supernatural occurrences of Jesus. Question all that it might of his virgin birth, his double nature, and his restoration. They may attempt to clarify it away all they need about Jesus mending the wiped out, sustaining the hoards, throwing out fallen angels or raising the dead. Philosophize every one of the one need about the life and teachings of Christ. Some people let question have its direction. However, I know for myself that Jesus is genuine! How would I know he's genuine? I can feel him path wear in my spirit.

There's one and only truth why Jesus is not overlooked. One certainty decreases to yield. The certainty Jesus the Son of man has power on earth to excuse sins. Jesus excuses us of our wrongdoings as just He is God. No one but Jesus can do what he does being God who is capable.

There are people lost in their transgression yet I heard the Bible say: All have trespassed and missed the mark concerning the transcendence of God. I am so happy the Lord spared my spirit and pardoned my transgressions. There might be somebody here today who don't have the foggiest idea about that the Lord is tolerant, or that the Lord is generous, that the Lord is moderate to outrage however ample in benevolence. Simply request that the Lord spare your spirit and pardon you your wrongdoings and he will. Simply request that the Lord make in me a perfect heart. You can ask the Lord restore in me the right soul and Jesus will pardon all. Just Jesus is the response for this transgression wiped out world.

SERMON

FIVE

Who Is Jesus Christ?
(Matthew 16:16)

"And Simon Peter answered and said, Thou art the Christ, The Son of the Living God" (v.16).

Through many years there has been much talk and discussion about the who the Lord Jesus is. Many have asked: "Who Is Jesus Christ?" Who is this one who claims the attention of the world?

Who is this compelling man who has touched the hearts of such a variety of thousands or a large number of individuals through the ages? There has been numerous perspectives about Jesus. Some society today say that Jesus was insane or that he was frantic, crazy that he was allied with Satan, sovereign of demons. In any case, those of utilization who know and cherish Him say that Jesus is precisely what and all He guaranteed to be: Jesus the Christ, the Son of The Living God. The Bible says, one day he called his followers to him and said to them, whom do men say that I The Son of man am? They said to Jesus: Some say you are John the baptist or Jeremiah. Some say you are Elijah and others Jeremiah. Also, Jesus asked them however whom do you say that I am?

Here it is that Peter, the representative for the gathering said: "Thou workmanship the Christ, The Son of The Living God." This answer satisfied Jesus and Jesus said, "Fragile living creature and blood hath not uncovered it unto thee, but rather my Father which is in paradise."

In today's sermon it is difficult to let you know everything about Jesus. Not in one sermon, nor countless sermons lectured over many years. Why? Since his decency, affection and who he is far surpasses every one of the books and original copies expounded on him. His kindness, elegance and pardoning forever surpasses the entirety of each good thing talked about Him.

Today, we can talk about on some of his high indicates as we attempt answer the age old inquiry, who is Jesus Christ? As a matter of first importance Jesus is a heavenly individual. His eternal is appeared by his life. Jesus was conceived of a virgin. A heavenly attendant advises her that God is going to utilize her to bring his own Son into the world. Jesus did not have a human a father. Jesus was supernaturally brought about by the Holy Spirit, and there has never been and will never be another birth this way. Here, God infringes upon the laws of human heredity. The introduction of Jesus demonstrates to us that God isn't liable to human or physical constraints. We wonder about Jesus birth and we can't clarify it outside the awesome extraordinary force of God.

In Genesis 18:14 we read: "Is anything too hard for God?" He had the ability to infringe upon down earth's characteristic laws and cause his child to be conceived of a virgin.

Jesus had a pure character. In the first place Peter 2:22 says: "Who did no wrongdoing, nor was cunning found in his mouth." Hebrews 4:15 says: "For we have not a consecrated minister which can not be touched with the sentiment our infirmities; however was in all focuses enticed like as we, yet without transgression."

There have been numerous great men on the planet however none has impeccable like Jesus. Each man that has ever lived has trespassed. Every one of the holy people in radiance had trespassed; yet there was no transgression in Jesus. Sin isolates one from God, yet Jesus had an unbroken cooperation with God since he did no transgression. Nobody would ever say that Jesus talked, thought or acted wickedly. Jesus carried on with a pure life. We need to say like Pilate said: "I discover no issue in Him."

The Bible proclaims that Jesus likewise performed unheard of marvels. Jesus offered sight to the visually impaired. Jesus brought on the weak to walk, and the hard of hearing to listen, and offered life to the dead.

Nicodemus said one night, "No man can do these wonders aside from God be with Him." Nicodemus was correct in light of the fact that Jesus is an awesome individual.

The world has seen numerous who case to perform enchantment however there has never been any individual who could perform marvels, Only Jesus! Jesus passed on a conciliatory demise. Numerous individuals all through history have made their penances, yet none as incredible a penance as Jesus made. Life was sweet to Jesus, yet the salvation of the world was sweeter.

Love is one of God's awesome properties, and he demonstrated forward his adoration in surrendering his life. Jesus kicked the bucket not on account of he needed to. Not on account of he demand to bite the dust but rather in light of the fact that he adored us with a heavenly love. The hoodlum on the cross perceived how Jesus kicked the bucket and said, "Ruler, recall that me." The commander of the warriors perceived how Jesus passed on and said, "Really, this man was the Son of God." You and I look upon his demise and say, "More prominent affection hath no man than this..." Jesus additionally became alive once again. His revival peaks each case made for his heavenly nature. No man however Jesus has ever become alive once again under his own particular force. Jesus vanquished demise and the grave since he was divine. Jesus additionally rose to paradise. On Mount Olive he brought his hands up in a gift. A cloud encompassed Jesus and upon the chest of that cloud Jesus did a reversal to the Father from whence he came. Jesus did not go down to rest in a grave as other men do, yet he climbed the starry statures on wings of force since he was divine. Who is Jesus Christ?

He is the special case who was conceived of a virgin birth, carried on with a perfect life, performed unbelievable wonders and kicked the bucket a conciliatory demise. He became alive once again and rose upon high. Jesus should to be sure be the perfect Son of God. His heavenly nature is appeared by his own particular cases. Jesus existed with the Father before the establishment of the world.

In the seventeenth Chapter of John, Jesus in an extraordinary supplication discussed the greatness he had with the father before the world started. Over in John chapter 1, vv. 1 and 2 Jesus was with the Father before the world was made. The Bible says in John 1:1, "at the outset was the word, and the word was with God, and the Word was God." "The same was in the first place with God: He that hath seen me hath seen the Father." Jesus came uncovering the character of God.

Jesus said, I am God revealed. I am God in the substance. I have come practical that man may discover and know The Holy one of Heaven. Jesus is the stand out ready to pardon sins. Nobody can do that aside from god however Jesus Christ being God took this upon Himself.

While Jesus was lecturing one day, a man was let down in his nearness from the rooftop top. Jesus said to the man, Thy sins be excused thee. Quickly, the Pharisees started to mumble, saying, No man can excuse sin however God. For probably the first time they were correct however all together for Jesus too demonstrate that He was God; Jesus said, are you sins pardoned as well as ascend and walk. No man can excuse sin aside from God and Jesus pardoned sin so in this manner Jesus is God.

Jesus is Judge of the world. Jesus asserted to be Judge of the world and this awesome capacity can not be guaranteed by anybody other than God. God has 3 strong capacities.

He is The God of Creation, He is the God off Preservation, and He is the God of Judgment. These 3 incredible capacities were all guaranteed and exercised by Jesus. We must admit that Jesus is divine. Jesus is the greatest miracle for mankind. Who is Jesus Christ? He is the Divine Son of the Divine Father. He is God come down to the world in the flesh.

In the first chapter of John verse 14 we read: "The Word was made substance." Lets take a gander at a portion of the evidence that Jesus Christ is God. Firstly, The same names were utilized of Jesus likewise were utilized of God.

In Isaiah 44:6, God is talking and God says in regards to himself: "I am the First, and I am The Last." In Revelation 22:13 Jesus say of Himself: "I am...The First and The Last. In Psalm 24 we hear this inquiry: "Who is the King of Glory?" and the answer return: "The Lord of Hosts, He is The King of Glory." In 1 Corinthians 2:8 we read that "they executed The Lord of Glory."

All through the Bible God and Jesus are discussed as One, (the same). In Romans 9:5: "Christ is over all, God favored for ever." God has five clear traits and Jesus has every one of them. God is Omnipotent and Jesus likewise is Omnipotent. Supreme means all effective. While Jesus was upon the earth he had all control over disorder, infection and demise; All control over the wind and waves. Jesus is the god-like, all capable God. God is the all-powerful, all capable Jesus!

God is Omniscient and Jesus is Omniscient. Omniscient means All-knowing, to have all information. The lady at the well discovered that Jesus knew the privileged insights of her heart. God is the special case who has all information. Along these lines, we realize that Jesus Christ is the All-knowing God. God is ubiquitous. Inescapable means He is all over the place and in all spots, present in the meantime. This is valid for Jesus! Jesus said any place 2 or 3 are assembled in my name I am in the middle. Jesus said He will be with each Christian all around, even unto the apocalypse. Jesus is at all spots at all times! Jesus is the Ever-Present God. God is Eternal. In Genesis 1:1, we discover these words: "first and foremost God..." In John 1:1 we find: "at the outset was the Word." Moses said, "I AM hath sent me." Jesus said, before Abraham was, I AM. Jesus Christ is the Eternal God. God is Immutable. Permanent means He Never Changes, additionally Jesus is Immutable in light of the fact that He never shows signs of change.

The Bible announces Jesus is the same yesterday, today, and for ever. Jesus is the Unchanging God. Jesus is the Only One True and Living God.

He made us. He protects us. Only he pardons our wrongdoings. Only he will raises us up from the dead. Only he will change our bodies. Only he will Judge our lives since only he give Eternal Life. Jesus alone is qualified to be applauded, qualified to be worshiped.

In Revelation the recovered hosts of paradise

worshiped the Lamb even as they worshiped The Father. In Hebrews 1:6 The Bible says "Let every one of the blessed messengers venerate Him..." Here Paul is discussing Jesus who is Lord and God the heavenly attendants are worshiping.

Who Is Jesus Christ? Jesus is a man (100% God /100% man) a genuine man. This is the place Jesus approaches each one of us. In some cases He may appear to be far away yet He is a genuine man and might be drawn closer as our dearest companion. Jesus had a human guardian. Luke 2:7 says that "she (Mary) delivered her first conceived Son." Although Jesus was powerfully imagined, He was Mary's child. Mary was really His mom as God was His Father. Jesus had a human guardian as genuinely as he had a celestial guardian. With a specific end goal to approach us and to help us in each need, Jesus needed to likewise be human.

Jesus had a human physical nature. the Bible says that Jesus got ravenous, parched, He cried, had empathy, He celebrated, He endured, He kicked the bucket and He was covered. so Jesus had a physical body and a rel physical human instinct. Since He was likewise human, He thoroughly understands our human instinct and its sufferings and enticements. Jesus was the main flawless and complete person who ever lived. When you endure simply recollect that Jesus endured and can comfort. When you are enticed, simply recollect that Jesus was enticed and can help you discover a method for getaway.

Jews 2:18 says, "For in that He Himself hath endured being enticed, He can help them that are enticed." Jesus was human with the goal that He could comprehend us. He is Divine (God The Son) with the goal that He could help us. In every one of the inconveniences, and considerations of life recall that Jesus is our senior sibling, our partner and our companion.

Jesus Christ is the friend in need of man. Jesus, "The Son of Man is come to look for and to spare what was lost." "Thou should call His name Jesus: For He might spare His kin from their sins..." We should thank the Lord God for He is our Savior. We had trespassed. We were headed straight toward damnation, yet in His wondrous beauty He spared us and made us His youngsters. What do yo look like upon Jesus?

Is it accurate to say that he is the Savior of the world. Is He your own Savior?

n the hearts of people everywhere throughout the world, Jesus is working through His Holy Spirit to spare what is lost. Jesus knows His kin and He is calling them by name. It is safe to say that he is calling you? Is it true that he is working in your heart? Try not to oppose Jesus for opposing Jesus is to without a doubt bite the dust! Who Is Jesus Christ? Jesus is our day by day quality and He gives us the ability to live. No individual can live without the Lord's assistance. Jesus is the special case who can give us energy to live as we ought to from everyday. In each one of our souls there is a yearning, a longing, a desire for a superior life. The universe of cash, notoriety, force and delight can't fulfill this aching (this desire). Jesus alone can fulfill our hearts and talk peace to our souls.

Jesus is the coming King. Jesus is King of rulers and Lord of rulers. At the point when Jesus backtracked to paradise the men in white said to the followers: "This same Jesus should come in like way as ye have seen Him go into paradise." Jesus is returning! Jesus is coming back once more, noticeable all around, to take unto himself perpetually each one of the individuals who have had faith in His incomparable name. Jesus is the King of Glory who is coming in eminence with His holy people to govern everlastingly and ever. What will you be dong when Jesus returns? Who is Jesus Christ?

Jesus is the world's last Judge. At the judgment seat of Christ, Jesus will judge the works of all trusting Christians. Likewise, at the judgment seat of the colossal white throne, Jesus will judge the individuals who let Him well enough alone for their lives. Each individual must face Jesus in one of these judgments either to be remunerated in paradise or cast out into damnation to interminable enduring until the end of time.

SERMON

SIX

Come Out From The In Crowd
(2 Corinthians 6:14-18)

"Be ye not unequally yoked together with unbelievers: for what fellowship hath righteousness? And what communion hath light with darkness?"(v.14)

"And what concord hath Christ with belial? Or what part hath he that believeth with an infidel?" (v.15).

And what agreement hath the temple of God with idols? For ye are the temple of the living God; As God hath said: I will dwell in them, and walk in them; and I will be their God, and they shall be my people."(v.16)

"Wherefore come out from among them, and be ye separate, saith the Lord, and touch not the unclean thing; and I will receive you,"(v17)

"And will be a Father unto you, and ye shall be my sons and daughters, saith the Lord almighty." (v.18)

A few months back I was driving not far off, turned on my radio and heard an old tune I had not heard since youth. It was entitled: I am in with the part of society worthy of anyone's attention. It said something like this: I realize what the modern aristocracy knows. I am in with the fashionable elite. I'm circumventing dressing fine; simply setting aside a few minutes, spending my money, talking garbage. We as a whole meet respectable individuals that we see and they make space for us day and night. We know we're outside of anyone's ability to see and made each lair around the local area. On the off chance that it's a square _ we ain't there. Young lady on the off chance that you are forlorn gone ahead and run with us. We will demonstrate to you a decent time, regardless of where you've been. You ain't been no where til you are in with the group worth knowing.

Presently, you like myself understand this is a common tune and it doesn't sound so well. However, there is a lesson too be gained from everything in life. A people group's religion tends to shape the thoughts of those it interacts with. God planned Christianity to shape the social world. In any case, today, I'm anxious about the possibility that that some of our kin have permit the social work to shape the ideas, thoughts and considering numerous in the congregation. The congregation ought to stay separate from the world. Apparently, a large portion of our places of worship get to be political minded, social minded and licentious minded; however we as a whole ought to be otherworldly minded. It is said today that religion tends to design after social patterns and social changes. Today, our social request has abundantly influenced our religion. As our social request changes, so does our religious expressions appear to change. I have dependably suspected that a country, a group, and an individual would need to have sense enough to design after their religion. To be more straightforward, their Christianity since religion could be anything and mean anything.

I'm no extraordinary savant nor am I a prestigious researcher however through otherworldly and prophetic perception one of the colossal issues in our houses of worship don't have the sparing force nor impact ti could have in our groups. This is because of the way that large portions of society in the congregation are out on the planet with the modern aristocracy. We need to think this way: "I'm on the planet however not of the world." Many are in the congregation yet they are likewise on the planet with the crowd of cool cats (the in crowd).

I heard someone say: Jesus Christ the same

won't keep going long. So let us not respect it. I hear a few grown-ups say that our young people are simply wild and insane. The reality of the situation is that numerous developed society are additionally wild and insane for the things of this world. A significant number of us attempt to stay youthful dependably while others are plastered with common things! A few of us need to stay youthful. No one needs to be more established. Everyone needs to be youthful and act youthful. I recall amid a Nashville affiliation meeting, an old woman who attempted to be youthful. This lady had on such a great amount of make up powder all over til the make up had splits in it. At the end of the meeting society keeping in mind people were going home; This lady was still situated. As a few of us passed her direction the lady said help me get up. This senior woman had on a smaller than normal skirt generally worn by more youthful ladies of that day. Somebody yelled out: Your skirt is too tight, you're all spruced up however you can't get up.

Everybody tries to stay youthful and use expressions like: "Each body else is doing it!"

Frequently time we don't stop to ask

ourselves regardless of whether we ought to or ought not do a thing since we utilize the reason that everyone is doing it. That is not genuine in light of the fact that other people is not doing it.

A large portion of us do a considerable measure of things basically in light of the fact that we see others doing it. Numerous society do things in light of the fact that the group worth knowing is doing it. A great deal of things are only improper in private and in broad daylight; yet some people do things

attempting to stay aware of the hip bounce of things, or as they say stay in with the in crowd.

Whether any other individual need to go to paradise or not it is an individual and individual choice. I need to ensure I'm going to paradise so I direct my life as per God's Word. Numerous behave to the expression of the world which prompts obliteration. I'm not going alone to satisfy the modern aristocracy but rather I will make the wisest decision to please God. Some society experience their lives just to satisfy the modern aristocracy.

Today, numerous young ladies who fancy a not too bad life are some of the time propositioned for grants or better employments in the event that they basically lay down with somebody. Some of them will offer their righteousness just to excel a tiny bit. Why? They feel they can better relate to the fashionable elite. Today, as a people we should be grateful God is a decent God. We should be grateful to the Lord for He has presented to us a powerful long way. Be that as it may, I am relentless perplexed a significant number of us have overlooked where we originate from and the qualities our fathers and moms attempted to ingrain in us.

In the event that a popular VIP comes to town a hefty portion of our kin will miss church that Sunday and spend our tithe on the show instead of be the place we should serve God.

Several individuals will regularly turn out for some VIP who has come to town and pass up a great opportunity for chapel since now I am excessively drained, excessively tired or excessively tipsy. There are numerous who pass up a great opportunity for chapel just to be a part of the group worth knowing.

You realize that the Lord has been, great to us! The Lord took us from out the donkey and furrowing fields for others. The Lord took us out from the old steed and surrey and place us in a portion of the finest vehicles. The Lord too us off old dusty and sloppy streets and put us on asphalt. The Lord removed us from broken, rundown, second hand houses and shacks and place us in Good homes! The Lord took away the old lamp oil lights that brought on so much smoke our eyes would tear. The Lord gave us electric lights! We should simply turn on the switch. The ruler took us from out old wood outline places of worship where the seats would or could leave a fragment in you. The Lord gave us pad seats and aerated and cooled chapels for our solace. The Lord took us fro wood blazing stoves and conveyed us to Micro-wave and electric cooking in our kitchens. These are only a couple to be aware of however all that we have originates from the Lord. Not the new aristocracy. Everybody had something to be grateful for. We should be grateful to the Lord!

shockingly, numerous individuals are complying with the methods for the modern aristocracy, the world. They invest awesome time, vitality and fortunes attempting to stay aware of the fashionable elite. Today, we have more than we have ever had before but we spend our well deserved cash on the great times with the part of society worthy of anyone's attention. I say to those people you better set something back for a blustery day on the grounds that there will be stormy days. The best thing I can encourage you is to discover time to serve the Lord. that as well as we take such a great amount of junk until no one trusts us!

We talk such a great amount of rubbish until spouses no more trust their husbands and husbands no more trust their wives. We talk such a great amount till chapel individuals will have a hard time believing us nor trust their ministers. We talk such a great amount in America until we don't accept nor believe each other however expect triumph with regards to outside discretion. We have to originate from amongst the crowd of cool cats and rushed to God. We meed for neglect common ways.

The Bible pronounces: be not fit in with the method for the world but rather be ye changed. The part of society worthy of anyone's attention offers you; yet Jesus offers all to you. He offers you Salvation!

The In Crowd says: when you are desolate go get smashed, have a bud. When you are lost hope or discouraged they say we should go smoke a gruff. Be that as it may, I say to you today, attempt Jesus! Jesus said: If you're weight and overwhelming loaded come unto me and lay your head upon my bosom and I will give you rest. Paul says: you should not be unequally burdened. Honesty has no dealings with profaneness. Murkiness has no dealings with light. An offspring of God has no dealings with an unbeliever. Turned out from among them. Turned out from the part of society worthy of anyone's attention. Be isolated from the world. The Lord said on the off chance that you turn out from among them, I will be your dad and you will be my child, my little girl on the off chance that you yet turn out from the part of society worthy of anyone's attention and turn your life over to Jesus. Have you attempted Him? You should attempt Him! I challenge you to attempt Him today.

SERMON

SEVEN

The Challenge and The Challenger
(Ephesians 6:12)

"For we wrestle not against flesh and blood, but against principalities, against powers, against rulers of the darkness of this world, against spiritual wickedness in high places." (v.6)

On the off chance that we take a gander at this specific entry of sacred writing; we can obviously see and comprehend that we are battling an otherworldly war. A war amongst great and abhorrence, God and Satan. Paul lets us know that for the offspring of God our battle is not against any physical adversary. It is against associations and forces that are profound. We are up against inconspicuous forces that control this dim universe of the earth and profound operators from the central station of fiendish damnation itself!

Here Paul was tested and went up against by numerous foes, however the experience made Paul swing to a standout amongst the most eminence challengers of all times. From rehashed encounters Paul found that there was a major distinction between a battling chance and an opportunity to battle. Paul says that "we wrestle." it is not a conflict as in football, which is coincidental to bigger developments by colleagues. Wrestling is not a strategy for testing quality. It is not the capacity to move under weight. In any case, wrestling is a firm fight between contradicting parties. It is an open field test with intense restriction. It is the challenger meeting the test.

In people in general field of Paul's day Paul had seen a progression of conflicts; thus Paul obtains "wrestle" from the games field of that day where combatants battled and passed on. Paul utilizes "Wrestle" to express his incredible contribution as a christian. Paul found that he couldn't pull back from the battles in light of the fact that the issues he experienced and the christian life lived in Paul's day was one of awesome troubles.

Our souls are a combat zone where great and insidiousness do fight. Inside our lives there dependably a contention amongst great and underhanded, light and dimness. Paul's encounters taught him that there is a contention amongst truth and untruths; a contention amongst servitude and flexibility. In this life we live there is a contention amongst affection and scorn, equity and treachery. Clashes have made an open door for wrestling. In the life of every christian there are clashes since we wrestle against malice. We wrestle against Satan. God needs some solid effective men and ladies who will stand up and not be reluctant to remain focused war zone as officers of the cross and battle the great battle of confidence.

When one moves into adversary region, or when the foe moves in on him, the challenger and the tested of need come to grasps. Every last bit that the challenger picks up the test gets to be more noteworthy. Dreadful men and quitters can never effectively meet difficulties set the christian. God's congregation needs men and ladies who will genuinely remain as christian officers.

You recall Gideon's armed force: Gideon's armed force of 32,000 was feeble to meet the test set before them. Later God picked 300 from Gideon's armed force cause these 300 men were not hesitant to meet the test. Gideon's men were more than numbers, they mean God. Each man remained in his place around the camp as challengers completely equipped for meeting the test. They were solid in soul and battled the great battle of confidence. Paul says our battle is against associations and forces that are otherworldly, controls that contrast in rank. All things being equal there is dependably somebody in the congregation who dependably seen to keep inconvenience blended up. Why? Indeed, in light of the fact that occasionally Satan impacts powerless Christians not to acknowledge authority. Satan impacts some congregation people not to acknowledge the test in their lives.

In any case, to shoot down siblings and sister in the congregation trusting that the congregation plan will fall. There are excessively numerous individuals in God's holy places who are only villains in mask. They generally continue something going. And afterward when God talks through their minister against the fallen angels they get most exceedingly awful. They imagine they cherish their congregation yet you can't get five pennies worth of work out of them.

They prowl up and down the pathway of the Christian. They say they cherish God; however shoot down each project which could have helped the congregation. Furthermore, when another minister acknowledges the empty church; quickly the snaps get together to make his life service hopeless. I am here to let you know that you're not battling fragile living creature and blood but rather you fight against God. Also, you should battle Satan with the good news of Christ.

There are some people in our holy places who have their dens in obscurity however put on a show to be hirelings of God. At that point there are the individuals who kick back and ask why is he lecturing that today? This is on account of God knows you realize that He knows you are the inconvenience creator, you are the damnation raiser. You are the feeble minded heretic and backbiter.

You realize that it is you who should be changed. You know it is you who is harming the congregation. At the point when the congregation may gain ground it is you who keeps the congregation down. Numerous may have joined the congregation - yet your sharp tongue got in their direction. There are numerous individuals who are two-timers. Now and then they are fake ministers who sugarcoat the gospel. They advise the congregation what they get a kick out of the chance to hear as opposed to carry out the employment. In some cases its an unyielding elder that won't do as he is told. At times it a choir part as opposed to singing for the Lord; they are singing for themselves.

Some of the time it is a misinformed trustee who as opposed to holding the advantages in trust, He's run not far off with it! Some of the time its a crafty scowling usher. Who as opposed to remaining by the entryway post and welcome parishioners with a heavenly grin they grimace and look so imply that the general population miracle is it Halloween.

These are yet a couple of the case of individuals who have torn up and executed a considerable lot of our houses of worship. regularly time these people have been in the congregation for some numerous years.

These society have been off-base here in the congregation until they believe they're the main ones who are correct. They think no one can be correct unless it is from their lips. At that point when adoring and minding Christians attempt to help them-they decline the assistance. At that point when somebody lets you know that God's pledge say else they get frantic and begin little snaps in the congregation. At that point reliable individuals started to leave the congregation and you can't comprehend why. It is on the grounds that reliable Christians need a spot to venerate in Spirit and in Truth! No one needs to go where there is dependably inconvenience or where there is an non - fundamental battle! No one needs to be around a mess of battling. Individuals' souls are shouting out in numerous houses of worship today; since they know as Christians we are not to search for an opportunity to battle but rather a battling opportunity to serve Jesus Christ our Lord and Savior.

Paul says: "We wrestle not against fragile living creature and blood:" that implies we are not battling the damnation raisers or the individuals who mistreat us, nor do we wrestle against them. Paul is stating that we wrestle against otherworldly powers of dimness. Our battle is against the person who impacts their lives. Satan himself, the underhanded one, Beelzebub, the fallen angel. Since we are Christians Satan makes a test.

Hence, we should keep in mind the villain or underrate the restriction. We should be that as it may, go to bat for Jesus and resist Satan. What's more, when we have done all to stand and the cause is great; the battle is not our own; but rather its the Lord's. The Lord remains with the individuals who stand undaunted with him.

The Apostle Paul had tired it on the cutting edge of fight. Paul had been abused, yet not genuinely harmed. Paul endured wounds, however not past recuperation. He had been stood up to yet not won. The restriction gave him inconvenience yet he had not been ceased by deferrals. Put all in all protective layer of God and stand up as a Christian fighter should stand. Stand up continually knowing we have a place with God and always remembering that we battle against Satan.

Keep in mind, Jesus is The Victory. Jesus met each test the distance from Bethlehem steady to Calvary's Hill. On Calvary, He won with his hands down nailed to the cross. He crushed each test. Indeed, even demise and the grave with all force in his grasp. Since he did the triumph is as of now won!

SERMON

EIGHT

The Prodigal Son
(Luke 15:11-13)

"And he said, a certain man had two sons:" (v.11) "And the younger of them said to his father, father, give me the portion of goods that falleth to me...and he divided unto them his living." (v.12) "And not many days after the younger son gathered all together, and took his journey into a far country, and there wasted his substance with riotous living." (13)

Whether it be consecrated or mainstream, this is one of the best romantic tales printed. It is a romantic tale of the extravagant Son. Here, Jesus recounts God's affection. He recounts God's understanding and God's' worry about man. Jesus means to demonstrate to us the perils of pomposity in the character of the child that stayed at home. Furthermore, in spite of the fact that he stayed at home - in spite of the fact that he didn't wander off-track like his more youthful sibling, despite the fact that he didn't take part in wild and crazy living: When his more youthful sibling was reclaimed he was excessively stoney heart. He was to egotistical to come in and participate in the feast. he was excessively self-righteous, making it impossible to participate in the organization of his lost sibling. Along these lines, Jesus plans for us to discover that it's unsafe to stay in the congregation and be stoney-heart and pompous as it is to go out and far from the congregation lastly return. Jesus means to demonstrate to us that God is the God of the lost.

Presently Jesus likewise said that God was not the God of the dead but rather a God of the living. By that he didn't imply that God walked out on you once you have passed on. What Jesus implied is that no man is dead with God. Jesus needs us to realize that we can not escape to wherever where God is most certainly not. For if man went into the sky and the most extreme parts of the earth; God is there. So God is the God of the lost and also the God of the living. On the off chance that you don't trust He's the God of the lost; then make up in your psyche to return to God. And like the father of the Prodigal son his arms will be open wide. And the Lord will be waiting with his wardrobe of blessing.

Jesus in this fifteenth section of Luke plans to uncover 3 things that were lost. To begin with, Jesus recounts the lost sheep. Furthermore, Jesus recounts the lost cash and Thirdly, he recounts the lost child.

On account of the lost sheep, the shepherd backtracked over his strides and his venturing to every part of the earlier day. The shepherd sought in each gorge and each mountain side; and each valley until he had recover the sheep that were lost. On account of the lost coin- the lady lost one of her coins. She cleared in each corner and behind each entryway until she discovered her lost coin. Be that as it may, then, There's no expression of anyone having gone out to search for this lost reckless child. For the situation of the lost sheep we have lost of property. On account of the lost coin we have money related lost. On account of the lost child we have human lost.

Individuals go out to recapture lost property. Individuals work twofold moves, additional time, and additional occupations to recapture lost cash. In any case, couple of, not very many individuals trouble themselves about attempting to recapture lost relatives or lost relatives.

As indicated by the story, this young fellow got to be fretful. He turned into somewhat restless with the control, respect, and standards of his dad's home. Potentially, the cherishing standard of his dad was a bit of disturbing. The home preparing and the home raising his dad expected of him was somewhat dull and strict. Yes, he was youthful and searching for energy and experienced uneasiness his own particular willfulness. His heart had developed cool an outsider too his home. He had turned out to be biting and stoney-hearted. He was outsider to the conditions, conventions and circumstances among his kin. The far nation energy was enticing him to come.

So he went to his dad and appealed to his dad. Father give me every one of the bits of good that tumble to me. His dad did not delay. He instantly separated his living and gave the more youthful sibling his offer. Furthermore, very few days He took his trip into the far nation.

The father didn't go off searching for his child for the young fellow was lost. I don't mean lost just to the extent ethics or that which is profound. In any case, he was lost to himself. For the record exposed that when he ended up in the Hog pen He started thinking clearly. This implies he dislike himself when he cleared out home (when he left home).

Sometimes in life, God permits difficult circumstances and troubles to enter our lives with the goal that we will get ourselves thus that we will wake up and acknowledge what should be finished. Some people who sit in chapel have experienced some intense encounters and they realize that there are times in your lives when you suspected that you knew it all. Times when you imagined that it was on the whole correct to be narrow minded. The main law of nature might act naturally first however the primary law of God's effortlessness is others first. So it took a little inconvenience. It took some difficult circumstances. It took a little ailment. It took the demise of a friend or family member or a little adversity. It took a little shake up in you life to help you to get yourself. The Prodigal child didn't wind up until he had gone the distance from a rich man's castle to a poor man's swine pen.

So he took his voyage into a far nation and he got to be distanced. He got to be estranged to his God, outsider to his companions, outsider to his surroundings and outsider to his local home. The wild blue there called until nothing at home fulfilled home. The Bible announces: so he took his trip into a far nation and there squandered his living in crazy living. He just discarded everything! Indeed, even his life had gone to the swines. On the off chance that you squander you cash one day you will need some cash. In the event that you squander you impact, one day you'll wish you had some impact. In the event that you squander your well-being, one day you will need great well-being. This intemperate child squandered his substance in crazy living. When he squandered what had been given to him then a compelling starvation emerged and he started to be in need.

You see - starvation are as yet rising and it won't not have been a practical starvation. Now and again it is the starvation of good well-being. A starvation might go ahead in your group profoundly so. A starvation might go ahead with you and not inexorably going ahead with any other person! This young fellow had gone to this far nation and probably get a warm gathering.

You know church on the off chance that you have an auto anyone will give you a ride. If its all the same to you have bounty cash most anyone loaning you some cash. Yet, in the event that the word gets out that you are down and out The story is very diverse.

For you see, this young fellow has now spent all that he had and there are many people ponder that it is so costly to be an individual from the congregation. I'll let you know this-it is more costly trail the methods for the world than it is excessively be an offspring of God. More costly on the planet than to come into God's home and give God his bit. For when you get with the group out there you're okay the length of you can create. For whatever length of time that you bear the heap independent from anyone else. You're good the length of you can add to the pot!

Be that as it may, when it get to the spot where you can not do that any more, the world is through with you and your assets are depleted. For whatever length of time that you are doing admirably and the length of you don't require anything; you can't rest during the evening for the telephone ringing free. When you get to be in need and you encounter a starvation in your life, phone don't ring any longer. Your companions get to be scattered.

This intemperate child was diminished to a dishonorable level in life to be a Jew. Just a Jew could let us know how terrible it feels to be secured to a gentile ace and living in the swine pen.

The extravagant child just sat there in the pig pen. He sat there alone and hungry. He sat there brimming with knowledge. He sat there loaded with experience that he picked up from every one of his hardships. He just sat there considering how hungry he was and acknowledged (in the wake of waking up) that he had com from a castle of extraordinary wealth down to a pig pen of life. Through this circumstance he begun to act normally again. He woke up. God wishes that a few of us wake up. You know church Jesus recounted the account of the intemperate child to tell us that he had confidence in men. Jesus couldn't at last trust that humanity was mischievous or that humankind was simply corrupt. A definitive end was for man to return back to God. We need to get on our knees and ask. At that point we should make up our brains to come back to God.

To do amiss with outsider with man. However, one of nowadays misleading quality and stoney hearts will pass away. One of nowadays childishness will vanish. One of these days of yore question will pass away. One of nowadays wars and gossipy tidbits about wars will all vanish. One of these peace will win. One of propositions days cooperative attitude decimate fiendish.

This young fellow simply satisfy there in the swine pen contemplating every one of that has unfolded concerning his life. He sat there in the pig pen. He sat there recollecting that he needed his flexibility from his dad's tenets. he needed Freedom from lawfulness. He needed opportunity from being trained and surrendered an upbeat home.

He surrendered a drop home. You should have the capacity to see him in the pig pen. See him contemplating internally: Here I am in clothes! Here I am in squalid clothes while my dad has an entire closet brimming with robes. Here I am with all my gold arm ornaments gone. Be that as it may, in my dad's home he has jewelry boxes brimming with wrist trinkets. Here I am with no accessory around my neck.

Here I am with no where to live. In any case, in my dad's home are numerous mansions. Here I am eager and starving while in my dad's home I had bounty bread; and bounty to share.

Here I am in a gentile swine pen, But today I retreating home. I have been off-base motel my life. I am doing a reversal home to my dad. I am going to tell my dad that I have been off-base. I resisted him discussing give me, however here I am currently in a pig pen.

Here I am presently, back at home. My Lord, I atone and I sorry for my off-base. I been lost in the far nation. Won't you pardon me. Simply give me one more attempt. Simply take me and make me what you would have me to me.

Here I am presently! Here's my heart take it! Here's my hands use me as you need. Here my eyes and here's my life. All that I ask is that you make me, simply make me as one of your employed workers.

SERMON

NINE

Why Does God Put Up With Us?
(Psalm 8:1,3,4)

"O Lord our Lord, How excellent is thy name in all the earth! Who hast set thy glory above the heavens." (v.1) "When I consider thy heavens, the work of thy fingers, the moon and the stars, which thou hast ordained; (v.3) "What is man, that thou art mindful of him? And the Son of Man, that thou visitest him?" (v.4)

Here in our text; as the psalmist views and meditates on the greatest and majesty of God, He also sees how man is a fallen creature.

The psalmist miracles to himself: What is there in humanity to make God have an awesome enthusiasm for us? In regular dialect or in casual discourse the psalmist is posing the question, Why does God endure us? (why does God put up with us) Give us a chance to think about the psalmist perspective of God's significance with the difference of man's hopelessly botched up history.

When we start to consider it we end up grappling with the inquiry: What is man that God ought to even to such an extent as notification him? What is man that God ought to be aware of him? Give us a chance to thoroughly consider this inquiry as I make three suggestions.

Above all else, There is nothing in characteristics of humankind to make God be keen on us. Consider the purposelessness of man! That is to say: consider man's nature of being insufficient or futile. This world was made by God but then - down through the numerous hundreds of years and era to era individuals as a rule have demanded running the world as though God did not exist.

Our reality keeps on sinking further and more profound into the grimy dirt. Man's cure is to have dialogs, syndicated programs, magazine articles, neighborhood, national and global talks in the would like to apparatus up some parity of force.

Individuals in this world are overlooking every day more that man in addition to man just signifies humanity. Simply think how futile and inadequate man is. Like water can ascend no higher than it's source, no more can man rise higher than man.

It resembles the distinction in a blend and a compound. In the event that combine salt and sugar and taste it, it is still salt and sugar. The salt like sugar keeps its quality and taste. That is a blend. On the off chance that we take 2 sections hydrogen and 1 section oxygen and include light you'll get water. Two gasses together get to be water. You have now altogether new qualities and taste. That is a compound!

Like science correspondingly: man in addition to man measures up to man, that is a blend! Man in addition to God parallels another creation, that is a compound. Something new! Something Wonderful! Old things are passed away and everything turns out to be new. Man left to himself go ahead from stir up to stir up. He overlooks God and goes on a futile pathway to annihilation unless God ventures in. Be that as it may, why ought God venture in? Why ought to God mediate? Why does God endure us?

Why does God endure humanity? Take a gander at the falseness of humanity. Someones has said: For consistently that man has existed on planet earth he has shouted out for peace on the planet. He sobs for peace in the groups, peace between people with clashing contrasts. For each guarantee of peace all through man's history, he has broken each guarantee to get alone with his neighbor over the world, broken each guarantee to love his fellowman in peace. Humankind has turned into an animal who just keeps an understanding the length of it is further bolstering his good fortune! At the point when that understanding is broken he accuses another person. This is man's mankind to man.

At the point when God made the earth and made man from the dust of the ground, God planned all things great. Be that as it may, man has taken God's excellent creation and transformed it's worth into a general public of declining good and profound qualities. Our reality has turned into a developing cesspool of social shameful acts, family disregard and tyke and also parent misuse.

Mn has brought this world into a parading carnival of wrongdoing, bedlam and wrongdoing also we live on a bundle of perplexity. I say, express gratitude toward God for those men and ladies who dread God and go to bat for uprightness! For without the congregation, our reality would be far nearer to the flicker of self-decimation it is set out toward.

We said before that man has taken God's creation and everything except crushed it. This is on the grounds that without God in one's life, human endeavors fall flat!!! Man has neglected to control himself since he is a miscreant and requirements to know Jesus! Such a large number of today attempt their own specific manner without the Lord in the photo and yet will just come up short. Why does God put up with us?

Take a gander at man's disappointment! By and by, he has neglected to control himself. Man has vanquished the aviation routes and the profundity of the oceans; yet he can not overcome his own particular fears or interests. More established people call it what it is "sin". More youthful people called it Juvenile misconduct while others call it wrongdoing, yet God calls it what it truly is. God's sees man's condition as a state of wrongdoing. God looks upon the endeavors of man and see sin. God sees more individuals dismissing Him than any time in recent memory. God sees whole groups going to demolish on account of man's fixation on medications and a large group of other unlawful acts. God sees those houses of worship that lecture just a social gospel. Why then, does god endure us?

In our reality man has sticks on to that old

reasoning that says, its you're thing, would what you like to do. This is the reason such a large number of society are not hesitant to take a risk at what could be disaster at life's' intersection.

There are numerous who play lethal diversions in existence with their lives and the lives of those they know, never allowing God to come into their lives to have any kind of effect in their lives or to work out their own particular soul's salvation with Jesus alone. They rather risk awakening in the city corners or ending up in circumstances they apparently can't escape. Basically, stuck in an unfortunate situation.

Why does God not discount the disaster area of humanity's wrongdoings. What is man that thou craftsmanship aware of him? The main clarification I know of God's enthusiasm for humankind must lie in God Himself. For reasons unknown just known not. God cherishes all of us disregarding our transgressions.

The Bible says: God so cherished the world, that he gave his lone conceived Son that whosoever believeth in Him ought not die; but rather have everlasting life. God cherish us since He is Love.

Presently, love is never mystery. Adore

dependably show itself. Affection is never quiet. Love must stand up of adoration for us! No alleged mystery partner has ever figured out how to hide love without a clue of it in word or in deed. Love must impart itself somehow. The best manifestation of God is Jesus Christ. Jesus uncovered God's cherishing heart in his illustration however Jesus demonstrated God's affection us in His diminishing on Calvary.

What is man that thou workmanship aware of him?? The answer is on account of God is affection and God adores us! Why does God permit a few tragedies throughout my life? Well, like Adam and Eve our high fate to resemble God requires that we be allowed to pick the wrong with a specific end goal to realize that we rather incline toward the privilege! God does not stop to be adoration since he has given us the ability to put our hands into the flame.

In God's adoration for us he tries to cure us of any such craving. The interim achievement of malice is a piece of God's procedure of vanquishing detestable and sparing the casualties of shades of malice. In this way, if God has permitted trials, tribulation and disaster in your life; it is on account of in Love

He needs to capture you in your course far from Him. In Love He permits a few trials to make us need Him; and to swing to him to give him a possibility.

Why does God endure us? God endures us all together that we may give God a chance in our lives through Jesus Christ. We should allow God to converse with us. In our private supplication life we frequently time do all the talking. We need to figure out how to stop, search and listen for God's Words. Give the Lord a chance to address us. Give God a chance to address us at this moment! He addresses us in the individual of Jesus Christ.

Allow God to rinse you! He kicked the bucket on Calvary's cross to wash down us from our wrongdoings. He bore our own transgression upon Calvary. Allow God to live in you! The method for Christianity and the life is not that we attempt to act like Jesus but rather that we let the Lord carry on with His life in us! With Christ in us we have the trust of transcendence. Does He live in you? Do you know his sparing force? Do you know His keeping power? Do you know His nearness consistently and consistently? Give your life to Christ.

SERMON

TEN

The All-Powerful Name
(Acts 4:10-12)

"Be it known unto you all, and to all the people of Israel, that by the Name of Jesus Christ of Nazareth, whom ye crucified, whom God Raised from the dead, even by Him doth this man stand here before you whole." (v.10)

"This is the stone which was set at nought of you builders, which is become the head of the corner." (v.11)

Neither is there salvation in any other: for there is none other name under heaven given among men, whereby we must be saved." (v.12)

Many folk have the tendency to believe that there is nothing in a name. Sometimes people will ask the question – What's in a name?

There are many people who believe this but I beg to differ because there is something in a name.

Proverbs 22:1 states: a good name is rather to be chosen than great riches, and loving favour rather than silver and gold.

So, this is why I say that there's something in a name. A good example of this is: If you wanted to get some credit and the salesman asked you for a reference, you give them the name of your reference. Well, if the salesman knows that name to be a good name, most of the time you may obtain credit because your reference has a good name or your reference has spoken highly of your name.

Now, there are some folk who have such a bad name you'd be better off not to use their name for a reference.

There are numerous names which case to have power. Numerous presidents, statesmen and other extraordinary men have been known not capable names. Some of these men and ladies could sign their name on a record and change occasions or happenings on the planet. The majority of these people are dead and we rarely hear their names any longer. Be that as it may, this name we're discussing today was executed around 2,000 years prior. But then, today, his name is still powerful.

Everybody talks about him at some time or another. Some praise his name while other speak against his name but we all talk about him at some point and time. He doesn't need to have his name publicized on TV or radio since he's Jesus in any case, whether people trust him or not. On the off chance that you have confidence in Jesus if does not help him be Jesus. In the event that you don't put stock in Jesus it doesn't prevent him from being Jesus! Here Peter says to us in the response to an anouncement, another by an advisory group of ministers and Sadducees: they doubted Peter's power by asking: In who's name would you say you are doing these things in? Dwindle said: Be it known unto all of you, and to every one of the general population of Israel, that by the name of Jesus Christ of Nazareth, whom ye killed, whom God raised from the dead; even by him doth this man stand before you entirety.

Nor is there salvation in some other: For there is none other name under paradise given among men, whereby we should be spared. Presently, on the off chance that you never need anyone to betray you simply absolutely never do anything. In any case, at whatever time you begin dong something great people will assemble a conference on you! There are times I ask why it is that whoever took this weak man that was recuperated on account of Peter and John at the sanctuary entryway; I ask why they took him to the congregation. The Lame man couldn't walk so someone needed to take him to chapel. They took him to chapel rather than the ball park where many people were. He may have somewhat more cash at the ball park. They didn't take him to the move floor or discos. On the off chance that the man can not walk he beyond any doubt can not move either.

Be that as it may, similar to a mess of us today, when we have done everything that we can accomplish for the fallen angel; what we have left in us we convey to the congregation. Diminish and John could recuperate this man through the name of Jesus. Whenever Peter and John had recuperated this man they were then called before a board. The board let them know: If you quit lecturing Jesus we'll release you. On the off chance that Peter could have talked our dialect that we now talk today diminish most likely would have said - If you had gotten me when I was in my preventing stage from claiming life I may have run alone with every one of you. Be that as it may, I simply left the congregation. I simply left the second story room and I been filled with the Holy Ghost.

Whenever, anyone has been loaded with the Holy Ghost they can recount a persuading story. When you're loaded with the Holy Ghost you can persevere. So here Peter tells them that this name, this individual that you call yourself disposing of on the cross, that stone that you set at nothing. You said it wasn't any great however now it the leader of the corner. I couldn't care less how huge you are or the amount you have; in the event that you don't acknowledge Jesus name as Savior your can not be spared. For his name is almighty. There is no other name by which affliction can be cured. Just at the name of Jesus would one be able to be cured.

The name we are discussing they knew before He would have been. Prior to his mom was conceived they knew he was. Indeed, even before that-he was known. He was known before his incredible, extraordinary terrific guardians were conceived. Daniel 3:24,25 focuses this out in light of the fact that the ruler said: Didn't we toss three Hebrew young men in the red hot furnance? All things considered, see said the ruler: I see four and the fourth resemble the Son of God,

So Jesus, the Son Of God was known before his awesome, extraordinary, stupendous guardians. Much further back than this John said: "before all else was the Word, and the Word was with God."

Many society don't accept there is a valid and living God. In any case, those same people who don't put stock in God may regard the name. They may regard the name so much that couldn't pay them enough cash to name their youngster Jesus or Christ. This name was given under paradise and also unto paradise. The name of Jesus is a given name (given under paradise). Christ's name is an extraordinary name in paradise as well as an incredible name under paradise. This is a given name among men who need salvation; men who are going to die.

There is no other name than that of Jesus Christ the Son of the Living God, The Son of the Most High God. There is no abler name than that which can spare to the most extreme. There is no surer name than that which has been given for this reason.

We find that Christ name is the end of the law for exemplary nature, the wellspring of the law is heavenly, and the character of the law is just. The reason for the law is great however Jesus is the end of the law. The end of the law for a cheat is a jail. the end of the law for a killer is a rope; or the hot seat/gas chamber. The end of the low for an attacker is castration or deadly infusion. The end of the law for a book is to train. The end of the law for a watch is to keep time yet the end of the law of Christ name is to spare. Christ has a high name and Philippians 2:9 peruses: "And he has given Him a name that is over each name." He has an old name for Micah 2:5 says: He's one of the Old.

He has a superb name for Isaiah 9:6 says: "His name might be called wonderful..." He has an illustrious name since Revelation 19:16 says: "He has vesture and on His thigh a name composed: "Ruler of rulers and Lord of rulers."

He has a heavenly name for Revelation 5:8 says, the four and twenty older folks tumbled down at his feet, and they said: "Thou craftsmanship qualified to take the book and to open the seals thereof..." H has a worship name. Philippians 2:10 peruses: "At the name of Jesus, each knee ought to bow of things in paradise and things in earth and things under the earth, each tongue ought to admit that Jesus the Christ is Lord; to the Glory of God the Father." His name is so effective til one day a writer took a gander at his name and said: All hail the force of Jesus Name.

The name of Jesus gives Salvation in its fullest terms and with the best conviction. His name is the main Salvation since his name lauds the perfect character. His name amplifies the perfect law. His name confirms the heavenly Word. His name qualifies the heavenly eminence. His name is over each name. His name is the power in supplication. His name is the focal point of Christian association.; His name decides over everything that stands for good.

For those of us who are Christians we should will to comply with his name. Like Abraham we should wouldn't fret languishing over His name. Like Moses we should be happy to escape for his name. Like Joseph defend his name. Like Elijah save his name. Like Daniel endeavor out on his name. Like Peter affirm in his name. Jesus name is so sweet you can taste it in the apple. His name is so fragrant you can notice it in a rose. His name is so adaptable you can feel him motel your heart. His name is the solution for our trusts and the solution for our petitions. His name is the appeal to our will. His name is the mettle for the frightful. His name is freedom for the headed and deliverance for the prisoners. His name is peace for the individuals who are confounded. You can called his name when your stuck in an unfortunate situation and help will get in a rush.

You can call his name when you are experiencing hardships and he will be there in a jiffy to help you through. At the point when the tempest billows of emergency thunder into your life, approach his name and you will see a rainbow of trust motel every cloud. Look for in his name and you should discover. Ask in his name and he will offer it to you. Thump in his name and entryway will open that no man can close. He's the starting and the end, the first and the last all in the meantime. Jesus is the almighty name. He is the past. He will be he exhibit. He is what's to come. He is yesterday, today and he is tomorrow all in the meantime.

Jesus name is louder than sound and faster than pace. his name is more seasoned than age and he's superior to anything great.

His name was determined by Daniel. His name was noble by Solomon. His name was examined by Ezekiel. his name was defended by Malachi. His name was scandalized by Herod. His name was confirmed by Peter. His name was condemned by Pilate. His name was punished by his foes. However, above all else his name is retained by his companions.

I heard Jesus was a zoo attendant in the Lion's Den. He was the flame boss in the flame furnace for the 3 Hebrew young men. He was the high sheriff when Peter was placed in jail. He was a thruway manufacturer at the Red Sea for the offspring of Israel. He was a funeral director at Moses burial service on Mt. Nebo. He was a rate cop on the Damascus street who changed Paul from a persecutor to an evangelist. He was the plane at Elisha's flight. His name is all my trust. he won't overlook your spirit. He won't let you trusts be lost.

Numerous people need to overlook the Name of Jesus. They took supplication out the schools. They suspected that would eradicate Jesus name. In any case, I am happy regardless I hear youngsters singing Jesus cherish me this I know.

You know, you can not eradicate his name for his name is staying put. The individuals who need to eradicate his name let me know what force would you utilize? I heard Jesus say All force in earth is in my grasp. In the event that you attempt to utilize fire it will decline to smolder. On the off chance that you attempt to utilize water Jesus will simply stroll on the water. In the event that you attempt to utilize the law then Jesus will be discovered impeccable for he is the satisfaction of the law. In the event that you put him in a grave he would simply ascend from the grave. In the event that you attempt to disregard him Jesus will simply whisper these words: I remain at the entryway and thump. In the event that you open up and let me in; I will come in and sup with you. His name is almighty.

You would need to pull up every one of the lilies since he is lily of the valley.

You would need to demolish every one of the vines since Jesus is the True vine.

You would need to impact away every one of the stones since he is the stone of ages.

You would need to chop down each tree for Jesus is the Tree of Life.

You would need to murder 13,000,000 stallions for Job said: He's a steed pouring in the

BIBLIOGRAPHY

The Holy Bible (1989) The King James Version. Nashville: TN.:Thomas Nelson Inc (Used By Permission)

The New Combine Bible Dictionary And Concordance (1984). Dallas, TX.: American Evangelism Association

The Holy Bible (1964) The Authorized king James Version. Chicago, Ill.: J. G. Ferguson

The Holy Bible (1953) The Revised Standard Version. Nashville, TN.: Thomas Nelson & Sons (Used By Permission)

The Holy Bible (1901) The American Standard Version. Nashville, TN.: Thomas Nelson (Used By Permission)

About The Author

The Reverend Dr. John Thomas Wylie is one who has dedicated his life to the work of God's Service, the service of others; and being a powerful witness for the Gospel of Our Lord and Savior Jesus Christ. Dr. Wylie was called into the Gospel Ministry June 1979, whereby in that same year he entered The American Baptist College of the American Baptist Theological Seminary, Nashville, Tennessee.

As a young Seminarian, he read every book available to him that would help him better his understanding of God as well as God's plan of Salvation and the Christian Faith. He made a commitment as a promising student that he would inspire others as God inspires him. He understood early in his ministry that we live in times where people question not only who God is; but whether miracles are real, whether or not man can make a change, and who the enemy is or if the enemy truly exists.

Dr. Wylie carried out his commitment to God, which has been one of excellence which led to his earning his Bachelors of Arts in Bible/

Theology/Pastoral Studies. Faithful and obedient to the call of God, he continued to matriculate in his studies earning his Masters of Ministry from Emmanuel Bible College, Nashville, Tennessee & Emmanuel Bible College, Rossville, Georgia. Still, inspired to please the Lord and do that which is well – pleasing in the Lord's sight, Dr. Wylie recently on March 2006, completed his Masters of Education degree with a concentration in Instructional Technology earned at The American Intercontinental University, Holloman Estates, Illinois. Dr. Wylie also previous to this, earned his Education Specialist Degree from Jones International University, Centennial, Colorado and his Doctorate of Theology from The Holy Trinity College and Seminary, St. Petersburg, Florida.

Dr. Wylie has served in the capacity of pastor at two congregations in Middle Tennessee and Southern Tennessee, as well as served as an

Evangelistic Preacher, Teacher, Chaplain, Christian Educator, and finally a published author, writer of many great inspirational Christian Publications such as his first publication: ***"Only One God: Who Is***

He?" – published August 2002 via formally 1ˢᵗ books library (which is now AuthorHouse Book Publishers located in Bloomington, Indiana & Milton Keynes, United Kingdom) which caught the attention of **The Atlanta Journal Constitution Newspaper.**

Finally, Dr. Wylie's *"Ten Great Christian Sermons-Volume I"* by a God-fearing man who is not only an exceptional, a prolific writer or inspiring himself; but allows God to lead him. Dr. Wylie is one of whom many think very highly of and is well sought after by many of his peers. This publication is a *"must read."*

73